QUENNETS

Philip Terry was born in Belfast and has taught at the universities of Caen, Plymouth, and Essex, where he is currently Director of the Centre for Creative Writing. His books include the anthology of short stories *Ovid Metamorphosed* (2000), the poetry collections *Oulipoems* (2006), *Oulipoems 2* (2009) and *Shakespeare's Sonnets* (2010), and the novel *tapestry* (2013), which was shortlisted for the Goldsmiths Prize. He is the translator of Raymond Queneau's *Elementary Morality* (2007), and Georges Perec's *I Remember* (2014). *Dante's Inferno*, which relocates Dante's poem to present-day Essex, was published in 2014 and was an Independent poetry title of the year.

T0170161

Also by Philip Terry from Carcanet Press

Dante's Inferno, 2014
Shakespeare's Sonnets, 2010
Elementary Morality (tr.), 2008

QUENNETS

Philip Terry

CARCANET

For Ann and Lou

First published in Great Britain in 2016 by

CARCANET PRESS LIMITED
Alliance House, 30 Cross Street
Manchester M2 7AQ
www.carcanet.co.uk

A CIP catalogue record for this book is available from
the British Library, ISBN 9781784102685

The publisher acknowledges financial assistance
from Arts Council England.

Supported by
ARTS COUNCIL
ENGLAND

CONTENTS

ELEMENTARY ESTUARIES

Blue buoy   Untampered simile   Black buoy
                     Grey water
Still creek   White knight   Cold stream
                     Red rubble
Grey sky   Yellow contamination   Blue sheep
                     Light breeze

                     Birds
                     silhouetted
                     on the
                     mudflats
                     lights
                     on the
                     Colne

Still buoy   Outstretched branches Cold sheep
                     Icy pool

Deserted paddock   Crunching gravel   Distant beach-huts
                    Azure sky
Retreating sheep   Anchored vessel   Sharpening wind
                    Flapping page
Uncertain seagull   Chiaroscuro clouds   Withering rosehip
                    Flapping crow

                    A shadow
                    points
                    across
                    oyster beds
                    A lone steeple
                    marks
                    the opposite shore

Retreating clouds   Crunching sheep   Chiaroscuro beach-huts
                    Azure sky

Lone redshank   Lean sparrowhawk   Lone duck
                       Vandalised sign
White horse   Green armadillo   Startled pheasant
                       Dancing teasels
Burnt-out car   Decoy wall   Distant rumble
                       Vandalised sign

A dense wall
of white
masts
guards the
marina
Pikes of
middle England

Decoy duck   Green armadillo   Burnt-out pheasant
                       Inaccessible sign

Red Andros   Red Charmer   Red Camelot
                    Red Crusader
White Siskin   White Shadowfax   White Avocet
                    White Panacea
Blue Merlin   Blue Lucky Dip   Blue Vinney
                    Blue Haversack

                    Brent geese
                    bleating
                    on the marsh
                    Cows
                    moored
                    on the
                    estuary

Percussive masts   Pink sail lofts   Persistent scraping
                    Private members

Exposed wall   Isolated thornbush   Narrow path
                      Secret retreat
Lone fishing boat   Distant light   Locked hide
                      Black barge
Holy place   Quiet days   Restored chapel
                      White sail

                      Sea meets land
                      River meets sand
                      Sea meets sky
                      River meets marsh
                      Earth meets sand
                      River meets sea
                      Sky meets land

Secret light   Quiet path   Distant light
                      Holy retreat

Calling gull   Uncertain yapping   Calling lapwing
                      Dangerous parking
Corroded hull   Eroded track   Gnarled trunk
                      Distinctive marking
Elevated nest   Shored boat   Abandoned bark
                      Forlorn barking

                      Oak trees
                      lining
                      the shore
                      Marram grass
                      stump
                      anchor
                      oar

Corroded marking   Private shore   Exposed roots
                      Forlorn parking

Bright-edged sword Golden-hilted sword   Broad sword
                    Slender spear
Shield-wall   Hearth-troop   Linden-shields
                    Life-house
White sky   Grey sky   Indifferent sky
                    Narrow causeway

                    Broken the waters
                    the ground
                    the hearts
                    Broken the spears
                    the pride
                    the shield-wall
                    Broken the verses

Slender causeway   Fated men   Indifferent sky
                    Broken verses

Banking jet Talkative cyclists Orange catamaran
Distant castle
Sprinting dog Obedient dog Trotting dog
Distant smog
Grazing godwit Purple marsh Languorous lapwing
Distant chimneys

Beyond the
bright reedcrest
two muddy
redshanks
patrol
the muddy
banks

Sprinting dog Purple lapwing Distant dog
Talkative birdwatchers

Airborne engine Still water Unpredicted wind-chill
Linear shadow
Airborne swans Calling swans Creaking swans
Squeaking gate
Turbulent waters Whistling wind Dispersing foam
Anchored dome

Marked out with buoys
illuminated by sunlight
the watery
runway of
two swans
coming in
to land

Enduring love Anchored foam Kissing gate
Mobile home

Winding track	Windy track	Wintery track
	Windswept gorse	
Shaven ditch	Electric fencing	Blighted crop
	Spent cartridge	
Abandoned vessel	Makeshift raft	Motionless barge
	Gutted pillbox	

A broken-winged
seagull
slips into a
ditch for safety
Now it is
really
stuck

Forlorn calling	Distant steeple	Lone magpie
	Spent cartridge	

Abandoned wheel	Yellow effluent	Abandoned trolley
	Purple tree	
Red pipe	Explosive flight	Mustard lichen
	Idle cormorant	
Red slagheap	Pink slagheap	Sandy slagheap
	Colourful sign	
	Two trees	
	struck by	
	lightning	
	branches raised	
	in supplication	
	The prayer	
	before the blast	
Pastoral image	Steel fence	Colourful housing
	Concrete reality	

Suffused light

Green triangle

Still boats

Oyster pit
Persistent warble
Discarded net
Blue Harmony
Bird call
Reflected sky

Squat tree

Oyster shells

Wind calm

A few cigarette butts
A few crisp packets
A few tin cans –
Skol, Diet Coke,
Beck's, Budweiser,
Fanta, Guinness,
Carlsberg, Dr Pepper

Persistent warble

Epstein mud
Constable sky

Suffused harmony

Distant droning   Eroding cliff   Corroding anchor
Burst balloon

Red grass   Green grass   Yellow grass
Brown grass

Bounding dog   Heiroglyphic marsh   Submerged tray
White feather

Abandoned
pillboxes
guard
the beach
Oystercatchers
patrol
the mudflats

Broken twig   White sail   Shark's tooth
White male

Hovering sparrowhawk   Gliding heron   Crow shadow
                          Abandoned tyre
Sprained ankle   Dead shag   Distant track
                          Marbled pool
Startled wren   Chocolate marsh   Deep water
                          Reed river

                          A line of blasted
                          trees stretches
                          out into the
                          heart of the
                          salt marsh
                          Epitaph to a
                          failed project

Barking dog   Hovering shadow   Startled track
                          Dead water

Sinking crane   Luminous soil   Tilted buoy
                       Stooping sparrowhawk
Piercing call   Abandoned chair   Icy gust
                       Diving shag
Red leaf   Blue boat   Yellow arrow
                       Barbed water

                       The smack's
                       russet sail
                       metamorphoses wind
                       into motion
                       The song of the
                       skylark hovers
                       over the ocean

Sinking boat   Luminous water   Tilted call
                       Piercing gust

Meandering crow	Flowering blackthorn	Nascent saplings
	Deserted hide	
Wintering bales	Spongy track	Offshore gales
	Desiccated leaf	
Gravel crunch	Sculpted pool	Spring sandwort
	Red earth	

Driftwood
plastic
cans
polystyrene
Print of dog
feather of goose
skylark warbling

Wintering hide	Sculpted blackthorn	Deserted pool
	Offshore crow	

Percussive creek   Beached hull   Snacking crow
        Saluting sail
Yellow boat   Sunlit shore   Gurgling tide
        Crumbling shore
Luminescent blackthorn Cracked earth   Aggressive bee
        Camouflaged tent

Rumble of
Spitfire across
the marsh
Banking
looping
climbing
swooping

Aggressive shore Camouflaged bee Sunlit crow
        Luminescent creek

Jellied eels   Illegible warning   Distant castle
                      Racing ducks
Cuckoo call   Parsimonious rainfall   Blue train
                      Phallic chimneys
Isolated spot   Lowing cattle   Suspicious greeting
                      Banking helicopter

                      White egrets
                      sift the mudflats
                      A hand
                      tightens
                      on the
                      rape
                      alarm

Toy stuka   Isolated spot   Mock dogfight
                      Distant castle

Postmodern town   Perished galosh   Feathery bulrush
                                Dandelion clock
Unlet units   Floating bale   Barge skeleton
                                Bland town
Archaeological features   Roman salt   Walking runner
                                Asda lung

                                Careful management
                                of grassland
                                protects anthills
                                The trees' teeth
                                decay on the
                                jaw of the
                                horizon

Unlet bulrush   Postmodern lung   Dandelion town
                                Archaeological galosh

Ditch litter   Inquisitive horse   Gliding swallows
                      Snorting horse
Red boat   Waterlogged sock   Distant steeples
                      Absorbent footwear
Infantile laughter   Earth island   Darkening sky
                      Deep excavations

                      Trade winds
                      carry plastic
                      bags from
                      the landfill
                      site across
                      the waters –
                      witches' knickers

Snorting swallows   Inquisitive footwear   Ditched sky
                      Infantile excavation

Colourful beach-huts   Sticky flax   Still barge
                         Broken shell
Purple clover   Cut reeds   Pink clover
                         Smooth egg
White mustard   Dancing cow parsley   Yellow boat
                         Russet sail

                         Shiny
                         black
                         ribbed
                         slug
                         crossing
                         the
                         path

Colourful reeds   Sticky shell   Still flax
                         Russet sail

Still pool

Blue shell

Yellow gorse

Colourful sails
Vapour trail
Squashed beetle
Pool shadow
Salty shore
Still pool

Lip of mussel

Razor shell

White butterfly

Sunlight
on
water
Mother of pearl
driftwood
shingle
distant laughter

Colourful sails

Blue mussel
Vapour trail

Still shadow

Isolated reader   Mown track   Soaring swallows
                     Grey dinghy
Waterside garden   Overgrown path   Diminutive dogs
                     Pink cottages
Private quay   Pink thrift   Adventurous cat
                     Terracotta buoy

                     A rusting
                     footbridge
                     spans
                     the water
                     Planks lead
                     into the
                     marsh

White rose   Black houseboat   Fluttering page
                     Diminutive garden

Blue butterfly   White rose   Purple clover
                        Black-headed gull
Fluttering butterfly   Brown dog   Soaring buzzard
                        Black pollen
Pink thorn   Sticky heat   Marsh harrier
                        Ruddy duck

                        Pursued by
                        birdwatchers
                        with telescopic
                        lenses
                        we struck out
                        across the
                        mudflats

Pink thorn   Flapping swallow   Rare vetch
                        Black pollen

Bog oak   Wind gust   Abandoned track
                   Bright sails
Rusted carriage   Marsh map   Gull call
                   Bright dress
Bricked-up windows Lone oystercatcher   Silted water
                   Lone tower

                   If you
                   listen
                   carefully
                   you can hear
                   ghost trains
                   taking day-trippers
                   to the water's edge

Cast anchor   Distant laughter   Raised eyebrows
                   Bright sails

Bell peel   Leaf fall   Brown cow
                   Swinging tail
Absent elm   Fly buzz   Bivouacked cow
                   Nettle sap
Reposing cow   Synchronised bells   Flapping cow
                   Stern cow

                   Without
                   moving
                   they stare
                   you out
                   of
                   the
                   field

Coughing cow   Camouflaged cow   Swinging tail
                   Leaf fall

Blue water   Rippling water   Flat water
                    Murky water
White water lilies Moored barge   Deflated ball
                    Upturned boat
Bright water   Still water   Sheltered water
                    Navigable water

                    Sugar loaf or
                    upended swan?
                    Maggots
                    pierced
                    by hooks
                    fly through
                    the air

Dangerous water   Shadowy water   Ominous water
                    Shrill call

Unimpeded view   Strategic position   Magazine passage
                      Increased range
Intact embrasures   Adjacent bastion   Landport gate
                      Curtain walls
Cartridge stores   Copper hinges   Water pump
                      Continental design

                      Each gun
                      weighed
                      12 tons and
                      had a range
                      of around
                      4½ miles
                      (7.25 km)

Strategic gate   Intact pump   Adjacent passage
                      Continental design

Still river

Private slipway

Muddy dog

Pigeon coo
Red rose
Scorched grass
Yellow sign
Persistent wasp
Piped music

100 yards
ahead cables
stretch across
the river
Blue decking
awaits the
barbecue

Waterside villas

Pub garden

Gentle breeze

Private villas

Pub sign
Persistent wasp

Yellow dog

Abandoned bottle   Red admiral   Private road
                     Clipped hedge
Static swallows   Peculiar people   Peeling sightscreens
                     Shaved sea wall
Grey gunboat   Missing chair   Yellow crane
                     Cuneiform seagulls

The dog
barks at
the red
lawnmower
Is it
time
for lunch?

Abandoned hedge   Cuneiform crane   Grey admiral
                       Missing chair

Velvet mud   Airborne seeds   Smooth bank
                    Oscillating fern
Iron fence   Yellow transport   Discarded packaging
                    Permissive path
Reversing lorry   Industrial waste   Locked warehouse
                    Chequered flag

                    Empty blue
                    pallets
                    stacked
                    in piles
                    Profit margins
                    recorded
                    in files

Distant tower   Chestnut horse   Winding track
                    Perimeter fence

White canoe   Marsh pool   Dung scent

White canoe

Marsh pool
Bird call

Sea wrack

Red canoe
Turning seal

Sky loop

Thistle spore
Waving seal

Dung scent

Wind spirit

Fairy ring

Marking high
water in the
samphire forest –
crabs
seaweed
feathers
leaves

White canoe

Sea wrack
Turning seal

Sky loop

Blustery day   Misleading sign   Distant gantry
                Uneven track
Crisp corn   Pheasant's eye   Red tractor
                Turbulent shore
Colourful graffiti   Dinosaur cranes   Constant swans
                Crackling sloes

                Nettles
                whipped
                by
                the
                wind –
                hedgerow
                hydra

White clover   Red tractor   Chalky soil
                Distant gantry

Morning mass   Azure sky   Silent saltings
Low tide

Grazing sheep   Hovering dragonfly   Preening swan
Still windmill

Motionless gull   Distant power station Standing lapwing
Plunging egrets

Nets
set by
spiders
in the grass
beaded
with
dew

Darting dragonfly   Rising tide   Calling oystercatcher
Turning windmill

Still creek   Cawing crow   Lone walker
                        Wigeon pond
Rare ibis   Underground stream   Barking dogs
                        Private meadow
Salty shore   Retired ferryman   Furtive cigarette
                        Drowned sailors

A Thames
barge sunk
in the mud
slowly carries
its cargo
of seaweed
to the underworld

Still creek   Underground dogs   Furtive stream
                        Chill wind

Brown back   White head   Short bill
               Orange legs
Stone turner   Can turner   Bottle turner
               Shell turner
White breast   Dark marks   Broad neck
               Stocky legs

               Often seen
               turning over
               seaweed and pebbles
               along the strand line
               in search of
               small crustaceans
               such as sand hoppers

Stone turner   Glass turner   Bottle turner
               Shell turner

Biting wind

Dark clouds

Dry land

Hard rain
Alcoholic shore
Dried-up creek
Oncoming storm
Bloated bellies
Illicit brew

Prisoners on
the island
deprived of
the one
thing
they
crave

Exploding liver

Lonely retreat

Windswept causeway

Biting rain

Hard liver
Alcoholic shore

Illicit causeway

Castle ruins   Misty horizon   High tower
                      Circular kiln
Burnt log   Fissured keep   Spotted dog
                      Leaning tower
White stone   Scorched grass   Black stone
                      High chamber

                      A sparrowhawk
                      hovers at
                      eye level
                      face into
                      the wind
                      then
                      drops

Scorched stone   Fissured tower   Circular kiln
                      Ancient ruin

Red buoy   Lone walker   River swell
                  Pleasure boats
Tide pull   Engine hum   Gull cry
                  Bright sky
Yellow buoy   Wind rush   White sail
                  Distant sea

                  Wind-trammelled
                  fence sentries
                  eye up
                  the barges
                  A gull swoops,
                  hovers,
                  plunges

Distant sea   White flower   Long river
                  Silent shore

Leaf stir   Still air   *Chat bizarre*
                     Barbed wire
Mill pool   Gull call   Still creek
                     Ploughed field
Tide flow   Reed stir   Water glow
                     Lavender islands

                     Water
                     scrolling
                     the mudflats
                     undecipherable
                     hieroglyphs
                     of the
                     estuary

Silent boat   Reed stir   Distant poplars
                     Chat bizarre

Tyre track   Mud flat   Birch brook
                    Turning boat
River swell   Bottle cap   Dog bark
                    Monochrome flight
Black water   Still lagoon   Marsh warbler
                    Luminous sign

                    Disused moorings
                    flank
                    the Colne
                    Dumped mattresses
                    cabinets
                    bedheads
                    traffic cones

Security fence   Green water   Absent cows
                    Long cloud

Wave swell   Gull call   Boot print
     Foot fall
Tide mark   Pebble track   Sea wrack
     Lip curl
Whelk digger   Sea swell   Shell glimmer
     Mother of pearl

Beach huts
wintering out
stretched along
the shore
pitched rooves
primary colours
bolted doors

Sea swell   Luminous shell   Tide turn
     Numinous bell

Still water   Goose trumpet   Pirate flag
                 Stirring reed
Clear water   Goose bleat   Private helicopter
                 Flat vista
Blue water   Goose code   Distant shot
                 Clear sky

The clamour
of two hundred
geese
explodes
over the water
fills the air
then fades

Clear sky   Murky water   Stirring flag
                 Muted call

Flapping page   Autumn leaf   Stunted tree
                       Blocked path
Desiccated leaf   Black branch   Abortive walk
                       Polythene wrap
Lengthening shadows   Slippery step   Black dog
                       Withered elm

                       The sun's
                       disc
                       low
                       in the
                       sky
                       light
                       blinding

White moon   Copper leaf   Flocking birds
                       Ambiguous sign

Still river

Shrill cry

Mustering geese

Bright sky
Distant bark
Gnarled trunk
Winter sun
Private beach
Industrial horizon

Unmarked track

Obliterated track

Stilt house

The sun's
reflection
bounces
across
the river
and into
the pool

Silent creek

Straightforward jump
Sinking sun

Turning track

Deserted benches   Resting gull   Tilted boat
                     Rotten hull
Clattering train   Passing car   Found shell
                     Closed bar
Still masts   Cold wall   Empty bottle
                     Gull call

                     Prints
                     in the
                     sand –
                     dogs
                     bikes
                     footsteps
                     hands

Sunlit shore   Still boat   Echoing cry
                     Dry throat

Deserted park   Wintering barges   Sizzling bacon
                   River cry
Crushed hull   Wading bird   Christmas song
                   Distant shout
Assault course   Upturned boat   Shield clash
                   Distant thud

                   A bronze
                   statue
                   commemorates
                   the defeat
                   A can
                   of Carlsberg
                   at its feet

Deep mud   Spotted dog   Day break
                   Dense fog

Distant castle

Morning ruck

Abandoned moped

Chattering starlings
Smooth fairway
Wing squeak
Wind rustle
Scrapping dog
Yellow lichen

Skeleton fence

Red barrel

Concrete wall

A buzzard
rests
on a
tilted
fence post
head into
the wind

Yellow sign

White lichen
Hazardous ditch

Shrill voice

Green field　　　Blue pipe　　　Running dog
　　　　　　　　Parked car
Pink house　　　Yellow jacket　　Black dog
　　　　　　　　Muddy track
Erect pylon　　　Torn nylon　　　Upturned crate
　　　　　　　　Locked gate

　　　　　　　　Marsh Farm
　　　　　　　　Country
　　　　　　　　Park
　　　　　　　　Kids
　　　　　　　　screwing
　　　　　　　　in the
　　　　　　　　car park

Burnt plank　　　Punctured ball　　Torn wrapper
　　　　　　　　Winter rain

Corrugated barn	Open barn	Flat field
	Rusty windmill	
Blank stare	Grassy seawall	Purple reedbank
	Luminescent weeds	
Graveyard snowdrops	Pure signifier	Tall hedge
	Still glider	

Even the fences here
seem pointless
Dilapidated concrete
posts garlanded
with barbed wire
Between
only air

| Corrugated bank | Graveyard weeds | Blank stare |
| | Open track | |

MAUERWEG

Clear sunlight. Scavenging chaffinch. Bird twitter. Freewheeling bicycle. Cream taxi. Grey stone. Golden statue. Red elephant. Orange taxi. Large family. Passing music. Red light.

Amongst the tourists two dishevelled men make their way collecting empty bottles from bins.

Leaf litter. Back pack. Bleached hair. Blue sign.

Blossoming cherry. Tarmac track. Slow bicycle. Yellow bin. Hot sun. Gentle breeze. Wall stump. Giant weeds. Fat runner. Grey sign. Industrial landscape. Single pine.

A man walking his dog on the former death strip follows it around with a plastic bag and a garden fork.

Hot bin. Slow runner. Single track. Grey sign.

Grey stone. Yellow bus. Hot engine. Passing train. Slow footfalls. Turning wheel. Zoom lens. Black lantern. Green bench. Granite statue. Silver car. Passing plane.

Cyclists glide along the track where the wall once stood, past the Sony Centre, Starbucks, the Tiergarten, to the Brandenburg Gate.

Blue pushchair. Yellow dress. Orange bag. Turning lens.

Bornholmer Strasse. Augustana Church. Dorotheenstadt Cemetery. Hamburger Bahnhof. Humboldt University. St Lukas Church. St Agnes Church. Treptower Park. Gorlitzer Park. Shuldenburg Park. Rudhower Höhe. Südpark.

Arbitrariness of the wall: one side the Reichstag, one side the Brandenburg Gate.

Schönefeld Airport. Rosa-Luxemburg-Weg. Waldblick. Birkholz.

Lost keys. Prefabricated concrete. Walled-off street. Tall weeds. Improvised barriers. Barbed wire. Island city. Hostile border. Compressed rubble. Firemen's net. Upright dominos. Iron doors.

Marx, Lenin, Engels, Mao. So what?

Different names. Darkened watchtowers. Malignant eye. Hooded crows.

Careful design. Immaculate planning. Perfect finish. Uniform look. New technology. Old ends. Reinforced concrete. Hardened steel. Calculated height. Secure foundation. Cheap materials. Infinite cost.

Along the top of the wall runs a thick concrete pipeline: to *stop* the flow.

Careful design. Hardened technology. Reinforced finish. Infinite cost.

Worried look. Black shoes. Rapid texting. Bare legs. Active thumb. Short hair. Round glasses. Brown skirt. Bruised ankle. Paisley pattern. Stern profile. Tense grip.

The dog, whining, moves rapidly back and forth within the orbit of its retractable lead.

Relieved voice. Abrupt departure. Stiff walk. Satisfied dog.

Ghost station. Abandoned house. Dead-end road. Truncated track. Bricked-up window. Empty depot. Blocked path. Closed gate. Deserted office. Divided cemetery. Locked door. Disconnected phone.

Arbitrariness of the wall: it is forever *crossing* the river, that most *natural* of boundaries.

Bricked-up station. Locked path. Disconnected depot. Dead-end door.

Black horse. Abandoned shed. Makeshift allotment. Chicken run. Sprawling trailers. Furtive glance. Brown dog. Dusty truck. Unswept pavements. Punctured tyre. Black headscarf. Worn beret.

Encamped on scrubland by the death strip: gypsies. They live in clapped-out vans covered in graffiti, sit cross-legged on the pavement, which has become their living room.

Black glance. Sprawling track. Worn dog. Punctured pavements.

Forbidden supermarkets. Original theory. Skilled workers. Political prisoners. Metal ladders. Iron lung. Steel cable. Microlite planes. Imprisoned spy. Attempted flight. Public transport. Building sites.

Successful applicants wait a long time, the paperwork is complex.

Pension benefits. Original theory. Suction effect. Special trains.

Run-down tenements. Broken doors. Cracked plaster. Peeling paint. Graffitied wall. Rusting shutters. Crying child. Broken glass. Unswept pavement. Burnt-out sweet dispenser. Defaced sign. Abandoned car.

In English, roadside graffiti: 'FUCK THE POLICE!'

Broken plaster. Defaced doors. Burnt-out tenements. Abandoned child.

Intense heat. Burning sun. Still air. Diminished ozone. Welcome shade. Unexpected shade. Intense shade. Natural shade. Urban oasis. City calm. Isolated spot. Pastoral strip.

Under a tree a man reading: death strip at peace.

Intense shade. City shade. Natural shade. Still shade.

Pink blossom. Picnic table. Purple bloom. Portioned apple. Lush grass. Distant cyclist. Bent bough. Rustic bench. Tarmac track. Tyre mark. Tired clerk. Tree bark.

Cherry trees line the path: gift of the Japanese.

Tree bark. Tyre mark. Purple bloom. Pink blossom.

Semi-circular amphitheatre. Angular seat. Circular beds. Straight track. Birch coppice. Evergreen hedge. Annual beds. Grassy track. Pine climbing-frame. Cobblestone road. Plastic sunbed. Asphalt track.

Activity all round the Wall Park: joggers, sunbathers, cyclists, walkers, strollers, sitters, climbers, talkers, explorers, presenters, film-makers, drug-takers, boules players, pool players, childminders, unwinders.

Semi-circular hedge. Pine seat. Evergreen road. Angular coppice.

Historical impasse. Institutionalised repression. Command socialism. Persistent opposition. Party line. Municipal council. Lopsided economies. Better opportunities. Zonal border. Military instruction. Secret police. Suspicious mind.

Nazi prison camps, used by the Stasi to imprison its opponents.

Blind faith. Security system. Foreign ideas. Hidden microphones.

Unsuitable bridge. Isolated fridge. Narrow bridge. Blocked bridge. Disused station. Enmured station. Erased statue. Forbidden station. Foot tunnel. Train tunnel. Disused funnel. Escape tunnel.

The graves of children are cleared for the wall. Toxins from the landfill seep into the lake.

Unsuitable station. Enmured statue. Disused bridge. Abandoned fridge.

Leaning post. Upright tower. Stepped wall. Parallel lines. Dense undergrowth. Equidistant posts. Dark foliage. Transparent barrier. Warning sign. Ancient trunk. Outstretched branch. Hidden bunker.

A figure moves in the bushes: ghost of Willi Block.

Warning sign. Dark tower. Barrage of gunfire. Unnatural barrier.

Urgent telephone calls. Temporary aberration. Coalition government. Interim solution. Unknown quantity. Mass protests. Blue denim. Mechanical grab. Existing checkpoints. Daring adventure. Disposable nappies. Popping champagne corks.

When the wall came down, an Easterner was said to have returned six library books, borrowed in 1961. The fine, DM 15000, was waived.

Parallel lines. Free drinks. Paper tissues. Long-lost relatives.

Oncoming train. Divided track. Driving rain. Plastic mac. Broken wall. Silver birch. Punctured ball. Glass porch. Fallen leaves. Blocked track. Distant eaves. Chimney stack.

Swallows have made their nest here, in the hollows of the wall. They sing over the death strip.

Expanded gardens. Cul-de-sac. Evaporating rain. Tarmac.

Traffic circle. Clay road. Bicycle path. Petrol station. Smooth pavement. Cobblestones. Forest trail. Guard tower. Hiking trail. Artists' colony. Drug abuse. Asylum seekers.

Here, in 1986, Michael Bittner successfully fled to the West. Here, in 1986, Michael Bittner was shot dead attempting to flee to the West.

Forest abuse. Guard trail. Smooth tower. Asylum seekers.

Wooden walkway. Still bog. Dark water. Deadly nightshade. Winding creek. Blocked bridge. Wooden fence. Still water. Lone duck. Swaying reeds. Rippled water. Invisible predator.

Paradox of the wall: wildlife and plants thrive in the former death strip.

Dark bog. Rippled water. Still creek. Swaying reeds.

White tent. Red roof. White wall. Orange truck. White building. Yellow train. White tower. Green leaves. White spotlight. Blue sky. White smoke. Purple graffiti.

Wall spectrum: after the fall the colours begin to emerge.

Red graffiti. Green smoke. Orange leaves. Purple spotlight.

Souvenir kiosks. Single-storey shops. Media circus. Bored cameramen. Toy bears. Imminent opening. Tall scaffolding. Instant history. Free enterprise. Joint ventures. Transport containers. Emergency camps.

The satellite dishes are being fine-tuned, for the historic moment that doesn't come.

Abrupt habits. Television listings. Illicit traffic. Washing machines.

Leaping rabbit. Alert rabbit. Crouching rabbit. Bronze rabbit. Hiding rabbit. Inquisitive rabbit. Jumping rabbit. Bronze rabbit. Resting rabbit. Listening rabbit. Oblivious rabbit. Bronze rabbit.

Silhouettes on the border strip: only the rabbit could cross here at will.

Free rabbit. Diving rabbit. Bronze rabbit. Running rabbit.

Smiling faces. Aghast faces. Shocked faces. Speechless faces. Roaring faces. Struggling faces. Elated faces. Defiant faces. Tearful faces. Emotional faces. Hardened faces. Laughing faces.

November 9, 1989: thousands of faces, bouncing across the wall.

Puzzled faces. Wistful faces. Bruised faces. Jubilant faces.

Beautiful bridge. Light installation. Last defence. Copper bear. Twin towers. Red brick. Warning sign. Tarmac road. Exposed cobbles. Regular lamps. Parked cars. Passing train.

A weeping willow marks the former border crossing.

Commemorative stamp. Illegible sign. Regular arch. Calculated span.

River Wall. Wind rustle. White boat. Exclusive housing. Red tape. Orange buoy. Abandoned net. Exclusive housing. White gate. Window grille. Giant frog. Exclusive housing.

Behind the tinted glass of the conference centre, executives are instructed on how to achieve their goals.

Remarkable tiling. Locked gate. Private garden. Exclusive housing.

Silver birch. Narrow track. Long shadow. Distant cyclist. Bare branch. Smooth path. Partial shade. Approaching cyclist. Rough bark. Straight track. Bright sunlight. Passing cyclist.

Of the wall, not a trace.

Broken twig. Empty track. Passing cloud. Vanished cyclist.

Autumn pastels. Empty tables. Steering committee. Compass motif. Telephone tapping. Travel restrictions. Station lockers. Battered cars. Dirty secrets. Expensive surgery. Dodgy digitals. Private beach.

In the West, down by Checkpoint Charlie, Rostropovich plays Bach before the wall.

Underfloor heating. Tinned peaches. Transit routes. Tennis courts.

Exposed location. Watchtower foundations. Red and white railings. Extensive security. Turbine building. Intensive phase. Soviet generators. Continuous shifts. Power stations. Metal pillars. Construction department. Day nursery.

Lamps of the light strip arching over the trees: wall-ribs.

General hospital. Valid authorisation. Border troops. Perimeter fortifications.

Spiked discs. Urban void. Spontaneous vegetation. Garden allotments. Uniform enclosure. Sporadic remnants. Concrete pillars. Additional security. Southern firewall. Electricity station. Barbed wire. Minimal interruption.

Railing posts – Giacommettis – marking the restricted zone: wall widows.

Red and white poles. Abundant vegetation. Barren line. Attempted escape.

Evening news. GDR citizens. Concrete overhang. Border guards. U-Bahn station. Camera lights. Street furniture. Traffic lights. Embassy garden. Two sisters. Bone marrow. Recent arrivals.

It was enough for her. She packed her bags.

Tight circle. Close quarters. Touching faith. Anonymous offices.

Evident traces. Extensive landscaping. Authentic remnants. Permanently employed officers. Stone handrails. Former entrance. Used car lot. Particular significance. Tall lights. Multiple arms. Large installations. Serpentine passages.

Kopenhagener Strasse. Dawn. A man climbs out of a green skip, dusts himself down, and sets off on his day.

Immediate surroundings. Equidistant holes. Ornamental posts. Sharp turn.

Ground floor facades. Tenement houses. Extensive construction work. Archaeological remnants. Escape tunnels. Slight rise. Concrete bed. Last generation. Contrasting appearance. Observant viewer. New constructions. Urban trace.

A bald man haunts the border strip here. They say his hair fell out overnight when the border was opened. Now he forever paces the former frontier, as if in search of his lost hair.

Indirect testimony. Terminal loop. Former building. Young trees.

Dramatic escapes. Six-storeyed tenements. Ruinous front. New incident. Ghostly character. Emotional charge. Dramatic events. Mass escapes. Upper floors. Ground floors. Dramatic resonance. Symbolic significance.

Death strip lamp: praying mantis.

Symbolic incident. Ghostly charge. Emotional resonance. New character.

Blue sock. Blue dress. Blue sky. Blue sign. Blue T-shirt. Denim shorts. Blue hair. Blue trailer-tent. Blue portaloo. Blue crate. Blue bicycle. Grey sign.

The cock of a former Stasi officer lengthens as he steps into the blue movie booth.

Blue swingseat. Blue tarpaulin. Blue tile roof. Blue pool.

Barking dogs. Calling voices. A roaring jet. Bird trill. Barking dogs. Closing gates. Approaching footfalls. Grinding gears. Barking dogs. Bird song. Gun shot. The wind in the trees.

How different these sounds now, and when the wall still stood.

Squeaking trainer. Jet engine. Approaching voices. Scrunching leaves.

Different generations. Typical breezeblock. Visible emptiness. Official use. Passport control. Concrete pipe. Security measure. Fresh concrete. Individual segments. Wooden lamp-posts. Illumination devices. Burial ground.

Here, they say, after dark, the ghosts of border guards still patrol their sectors.

Gutter-like trace. Sandstone base. Extension lights. Sporadic imprints.

Command post. Various events. Historic ground. Older structures. Original lamp-post. Accompanying pavement. Integral part. Different generations. Imprisonment cell. Neighbouring towers. Assigned section. Corresponding places.

Weight-watchers, in brightly coloured buildings, overlooking the watchtower.

Eye contact. Lengthy stretch. Electric barriers. Common room.

Unauthorised persons. Sector boundary. Special status. Complete maze. Wire-glass barrier. Steel wall. Ground plan. Immediate surroundings. Soviet soldiers. Original location. Removed elements. Near future.

Tar-blotches on the pavement: traces of border posts.

Numerous arches. Dead escapees. Memorial markers. Extensive construction.

Extensive redesigning. Hermetically locked. Relocated elements. Additional indications. City wasteland. Public space. Whole area. Specific situation. Lateral areas. Punched openings. Architectural language. Row of cobblestones.

Taxi queuing on Potsdamer Platz: driver in the East, passenger in the West.

Surrounding context. Urban fabric. Glass canopy. Relocated cobblestones.

Military service. Busy activity. Good man. Hard structures. State security. True stories. Small towns. Fine life. Border station. Crossing point. Another situation. Absolutely still.

They came to the hotel at 3 a.m., rolled him up in a carpet, and shipped him back over the border in a furniture van.

Aborted escape. Small stories. Big factories. Normal guards.

Gentle curve. Gabled front. Slot-like openings. Vertical bars. New construction. Authentic remnants. Further remains. Political message. Consciously staged. Extensive wastelands. High-rise apartments. Lengthy stretch.

High-rise buildings competing across the wall: Cold War posturing.

Colourful buildings. Vertical bars. Gabled front. Window grilles.

Original whitewash. Steel spikes. Concrete bank. Spatial situation. Pronounced trace. Electric control panel. Healthy lawn. Evocative remnants. Pedestrian passage. White marks. Extensive clearance. U-shaped remnants.

Border guards patrolling in pairs: to stop *them* escaping.

Perimeter traces. Immediate proximity. Light fixtures. Labyrinthine terrain.

Political message. Spray event. Stale visitors. Inner city. Anti-scaling device. Prefabricated elements. Intended function. Undamaged condition. Earlier era. Spray paintings. Limited durability. Official murals.

Graffiti on the wall: two cartoon characters tunnel towards freedom, as another clambers over the wall, pursued by a dog. As the dog tears off the seat of his pants, he opens his mouth to receive the benediction of the West: a spit-roast chicken, from Aldi.

Illegal graffiti. Greater durability. Modular elements. Solid installations.

Fur coats. Drawing instruments. Cheapest class. Ten years. Jewellery department. False papers. Political context. False charges. False pretences. Economic crimes. Famous scientist. Short write-up.

We went to his car, it was cold, it was winter, it was snowing outside.

Trumped-up charges. New beginning. Short time. Bad awakening.

Concrete obstacle. Crossing station. Landing bridge. Massive installation. Extension lights. Immediate vicinity. Storage buildings. Fortified jetty. Unique remnant. Factory premises. Potential escape. Standard element.

Whiteness of the border walls: to facilitate shooting.

Electronic devices. Original searchlight. Directing centre. Panoramic view.

Significant remnants. Repellent details. Deep trench. Derelict land. New constructions. Urban layout. Lengthy section. Partially exposed. Traces of rust. Former connection. Moving persons. Concrete foundations.

Cigarettes on the death strip: Marlboro, Camel, JPS.

Former barriers. Clear images. Brutal transition. Rigidly secured.

Wall memorial. Urban void. Visible incision. Different structures. Enemy side. Horizontal bar. Small garden. Abstract element. Electrical cables. Interrupted row. Large terrain. Garage buildings.

Allotments flanking the wall: apples, carrots, runner beans.

Comparable remnants. Numerous blocks. Peculiar feature. Missing trees.

Bank reinforcement. Electrical switchbox. Last victim. High fence. Ten bullets. New construction. Special pass. Adjacent pavements. Lateral enclosures. Art installation. Humourous comment. Authentic components.

The gardener's ingenuity: stretch-metal fence trellis.

Concrete abutment. Rural conditions. Former perimeter. Additional security.

Shady track. Felled trees. Pachyderm bark. Cool breeze. Open gate. Crying child. Red clothes peg. Missing cat. Children's voices. Stuttering bird. Traffic noises. Major road.

In the undated photograph a border guard is inspecting a vehicle at the Stolpe border crossing using a mirror on wheels at the end of a stick, the under-vehicle search mirror.

Freewheeling bicycle. Shady bench. Traffic cry. Early lunch.

Contoversial discussions. Appropriate memorial. Contentious question. Permanent memorial. Heated debates. Surprising turns. Bitter tone. Delicate nature. Heated atmosphere. Broad spectrum. Fundamental issues. Different opinions.

Dismantled wall sections, autumn leaves.

Heated opposition. Contentious questions. New futures. Political standstill.

Hot dog. Large bottom. Sultry afternoon. Empty bench. White dress. Brown rat. Dismantled scaffolding. Orange bin. Slow bicycle. Falling leaves. Distant drum. Rustling breeze.

A fat policeman, on his afternoon off, patrols the Brandenburg Gate.

Young lovers. Distant memories. Pink stone. White butterfly.

Grey concrete. Evening sun. Sculpted blocks. Long shadows. Irregular blocks. Plunging tracks. Carved memories. Colourful shorts. Irregular shadows. Hidden walkways. Sudden encounters. Memorial walks.

Leaves falling on the Holocaust Memorial: sycamore, beech, poplar, olive.

Emergent forms. Sinking sun. Swirling leaves. Distant bells.

Lead sky. Heavy industries. Cut corners. Rising curves. Respiratory diseases. Main drain. Dying forests. Industrial base. Poisoned space. Umbrella organisation. Malignant tumours. Industrial plant.

Sulphur burns through the dead leaves and stabs the soured land: acid rain.

Heavy sky. Toxic cadmium. Brown coal. Contaminated overalls.

Hurried steps. Validated ticket. Missed train. Empty platform. Hot carriage. Cumbersome map. Confusing sign. Wrong train. Hot sweat. Retraced steps. Lost minutes. Hand-drawn map.

Ants running up and down the trunk of a plane tree: insect commuters.

Lost map. Labyrinthine building. Empty room. Shady bench.

Smoking commuter. Polished steps. Photo opportunity. Passing barge. Orange bag. Swirling water. Swept leaves. Brown bag. Pedestrian bridge. Green taxi. Grey railings. Gear click.

Outside: river reflected in glass. Inside: porters walking on water.

Passing jogger. Empty bench. Still water. Billowing jacket.

Special waste. Exotic garbage. Landlocked island. Unplanned events. Open slagheaps. Contaminated waste. Natural gas. Nuclear power. Heavy fertilizer. Industrial emissions. Bald patches. Bad water.

Hooded crows that seem to be everywhere, like the police.

Nuclear programmes. Technical equipment. Organic waste. Open-cast mining.

Rusting car. Deserted wasteland. Suspicious pedestrian. Colourful graffiti. Evening sunlight. Distant helicopter. Still water. Grey wall. Spiral steps. Squeaking pedals. Whingeing child. Red bricks.

By the Spree: a wall fragment punched with the letters MEMORY.

Passing siren. Rumbling train. Disused warehouse. Tired brain.

Neat gardens. Idle dogs. Polished cars. Suburban villas. German flags. Locked gates. Trim hedges. Closed blinds. Lush gardens. Neat patios. Regimented gardens. Straight road.

Suburban villas have replaced the death strip here, their facades like bunkers.

Gated communities. Hostile looks. Exterminated moles. Lush gardens.

Open meadow. Gravel track. Still creek. Floating plank. Low-flying swallow. Sandy track. Grazing horses. Pink back. Heavy hooves. Swishing tail. Horse manure. Cycle trail.

Above the trees, cirrus clouds, sculpted by the wind.

Horse snort. Tinkling bridle. Dusty track. Still heron.

Hot asphalt. Smooth asphalt. Scorched grass. Wire fence. Familiar lamps. Silent warehouse. Parked cars. Passing train. Tree shade. Resting cyclist. Steep gulley. Sleeping builder.

In the centre of the city, a tree-lined path: miracle of the wall.

Leaf rustle. Train clatter. Yellow bin. Green shade.

Future music. Window frames. American soldiers. Wishful thinking. White goose. Jib crane. Toilet brush. Corrugated iron. Poisonous music. Natural boulder. Small animals. Random violence.

A man who lives by the wall goes crazy. He flips, takes his electric drill on a long cable and starts drilling a hole in the wall.

Socialist heroes. Canine holocaust. Earnest walkers. Poisoned land.

Ornamental well. Barbed wire. Bolted gate. Ornamental rose. Covered pool. Overgrown hedge. Stacked chairs. Garden table. No entry sign. Badminton net. Trailing vine. Tall pine.

On the former death strip, four holiday cottages.

Pink shutters. Stacked chairs. Green shutters. Bright lamps.

Falling leaf. Telescopic lens. Calling gull. Lapping waves. Private road. Hidden gardens. Palatial dwellings. Barking dog. Fallen net. Gothic turret. Iron railings. Numbered trees.

A black and white sign nailed to a gatepost: beware of the cats.

Purple flowers. Secluded bench. Symbolic wagon-wheel. Locked gate.

Old TV sets. New formalities. High treason. Captive population. Used materials. Wickerwork prams. Giant frogs. Idealised peasants. Wide pavements. New flowers. Faded paint. False information.

Traffic: Trabi, Mercedes, Opel, BMW, Trabi, Trabi, Wartburg, Lada, taxi, one Fiat Zil with East Berlin plates.

Cement statuary. Totalitarian ice. Old habit. Red scarf.

Blue house. White gate. Green bin. Serious real estate. Red house. Silver car. Ornamental lions. Lakeside situation. Iron pillars. Decorative totem. Wooden house. Elevated parking.

A fat man climbs out of his car, crosses the road slowly, and farts.

Ornamental lamps. Window baskets. Parked camper van. Stacked logs.

Wilted sapling. Dense pines. Blue dragonfly. Noisy bee. Distant shouts. Serious cyclist. Sandy track. Hovering bee. Discarded tissue. Unexpected van. Waymarked track. Stout man.

When you meet Germans out walking, they never say hello, but walk past as if you weren't there. Why is this?

Aggressive bee. Straight track. Dusty boots. Aching back.

Calling birds. Dense forest. Distant crash. Nearby voices. Soaring buzzard. Growling dog. Broken chair. Thinning hair. Winning ticket. Cloudy sky. Twisting track. Dandelion clock.

It is the wall sections traversing Berlin's forests that most bring home the desperation of the East Germans, and the paranoia of their masters: even without the wall, the forests are so dense they are totally impenetrable, like the wall of thorns surrounding Sleeping Beauty's castle.

Barking dog. Mumbled apology. Gentle breeze. Impenetrable questions.

German flags. Honking horns. Football chants. Daubed faces. German flags. Bottled beer. Friendly greetings. Honking horns. Honking horns. German flags. Patriotic chants. German flags.

Football fans in their thousands marching to the Tiergarten for the big match.

German flags. Aggressive chants. Honking horns. Broken glass.

Foreign firms. Latent nightmares. Empty bottles. Wooden benches. Prime locations. Scientific knowledge. Public buildings. Social market. Fascist venom. First trees. Bitter years. Low rooms.

A border guard's booth at the Brandenburg Gate, converted to a postcard stall.

Plastic dog turd. Smuggled microfilm. Crystal ball. Old traumas.

Quiet morning. Sleepy suburb. Barking dog. Staring crowd. Worried look. Crying child. Contemplative firemen. Sad lions. Troubled look. Calling grandmother. Passing cyclist. High balcony.

Westfalenring: the fire brigade is out. In the gutter, on the sixth floor, a cat swishes its tail.

Coaxing voices. Indifferent cat. Metal guttering. Crying child.

Tarmac track. Scuffed footfalls. Shady track. Staring cyclist. Screaming jet. Scraping gravel. Ivy-covered house. Garden oasis. Turning wheels. Still water. Absent wall. Luxurious villas.

The ratio of cyclists to walkers is 10:1. It's the same as the ratio of attempted escapes to successful ones.

Present wall. Passing cyclist. Turning wheels. Scuffed footfalls.

Waterlogged ground. Rising wind. Tall nettles. Silver tower. Muscular cyclist. Passing boat. Black water. Orange buoy. Resting cyclists. Wooden benches. Old bridge. Recent traumas.

An old man comes running towards me in nothing but boxer shorts: what is pursuing him?

Barking dog. Turning car. Reproachful breeze. Yellow jersey.

Paper cup. Slug trail. Slow cyclists. Green bin. Border bridge. Memorial stone. Turning wheel. Mobile home. Barking dog. Blue sign. Still cycle. Warm bench.

The clouds in the distance spell oncoming rain, and I've left my umbrella at home again.

Quickening step. Cool gusts. Approaching joggers. First raindrops.

Straight track. Monotonous track. Afternoon heat. Tired feet. Forest track. Lost cyclists. Misleading directions. Distant thunder. Stacked logs. Heavy feet. Dense forest. Useful map.

Forest hallucination: a cyclist dismounts and metamorphoses into a log.

Swaying branches. Protesting feet. Monotonous track. Afternoon heat.

Long day. Walled out. Cold beer. Cool breeze. French tourists. American tourists. Japanese tourists. German tourists. Bald man. Black shirt. Blue scooter. Blue sky.

Tourists flock round the wall fragment beneath the shadow of the Sony Centre.

Long day. Walled out. English tourists. American clothes.

Slow train. Steel fence. Bike carriage. Hot day. Closed window. Open fields. Yellow shirt. Closed window. Airless carriage. Sticky seat. Next station. Wrong ticket.

Travelling to Hohen Neuendorf in zone C, I've bought a ticket for zones A and B: will the border guards get me?

Tense forehead. Sticky forehead. Anticipated blag. Closed window.

Straight track. Calling bird. Dense forest. Solitary ant. Blue sapling. Passing plane. Solitary walker. Hidden watchtower. Friendly walker. Black umbrella. White paint. Brown shutters.

A former watchtower turned nature centre: now policing the border, now policing the green belt.

Rising wind. Cloud cover. Purple rose. Dense forest.

Green sign. White post. Marked track. Fallen trunk. Hidden lake. Damp air. Mustering gloom. Green fern. Moss clump. Mosquito swarm. Quickening steps. Marked track.

Passing a lake, I am literally fighting off giant mosquitos at every step, at every other *word* as I stop to scribble down these notes. Insect Stasi!

Quickening pace. Shaking leg. Swishing hands. Hidden lake.

Tarmac track. Dark forest. Gypsy van. Parked car. Grey sky. Cigarette smoke. German hoodies. Parked car. Open door. Lowered voices. Fat man. Grey moustache.

Suddenly I'm in the middle of a drug deal. I keep walking, fast, but not too fast.

Sticky forehead. Racing pulse. Slowing pace. Lowered face.

Slow traffic. Blocked bridge. Heavy rain. Smudged page. Broken umbrella. Lidl supermarket. Old hippy. Pulled face. Fluttering flag. Parked cars. Wet bicycles. Abandoned tyres.

Ad for Route 66 cigarettes: a girl kneels in the passenger seat of an open-top Cadillac, facing backwards, looking at a man who fills the car with petrol through a hole in the rear: 'Join the ride'.

Slow traffic. Dark sky. Passing bicycle. Wet feet.

Empty tables. American voices. Cherry lipstick. Springfield Missouri. Oh my God. It's shameful. He's very white. Very Italian. What's his address? Religious dictator. Get together. Medium white.

And let me tell you, you should see how they treat their women.

Very serious. I never met her. It was years ago. He's a bit more relaxed.

Wet pavement. Persistent rain. Sodden feet. Chafing blister. Wet trees. Heavy rain. Passing cars. Slipping feet. Wet buildings. Constant rain. Gusting wind. Slippery cobblestones.

Monotony of the wall walk, broken by the unexpected: on a traffic island a house built entirely of driftwood, with a bell of seashells.

Heavy rain. Passing clouds. Wet pavement. Passing feet.

Wet day. Faded colours. Peeling paint. Crude graffiti. Posed photograph. Cracked paint. Obscured design. Graffitied hug. Decaying monument. Smiling faces. New future. Defaced art.

So many signatures on East Side Gallery – Joe 4 Beccy, Baz July 2006, Jackie and Marco when you read this we'll be gone – it is impossible to *see* the art.

Unnecessary signature. Crude graffiti. Erased memory. Unprotected monument.

Dense trees. Wild rose. Startled woodpecker. Fallen pinecones. Distant voices. Colourful cyclists. Sign shadow. Tyre track. Stripped bark. Hovering dragonflies. Cycle lamp. Dandelion clock.

A narrow strip of sand, like a beach in the middle of a forest – all that remains of the former death strip.

Sudden breeze. Spoken words. Hidden termites. Patrolling ants.

Broken beer bottle. Transparent stopper. Red screwcap. Broken trolley-wheel. Tic-tac box. Empty water bottle. Used kitchen towel. Pink paper bag. White can. Dried-out corn cob. Used S-Bahn ticket. Used tissue.

A pack of Camel in the sand.

Trolley skeleton. Twisted tissue. Upside-down mushroom. Colourful sweet wrapper.

Piled stones. Sculpted stones. Painted stones. Sculpted wheel. Wooden strips. Breathing building. Inner wall. Crushed stones. Wooden bench. Pink stones. Yellow stones. Metal strip.

All air and light, open to the wind, a building that inverts the experience of the wall.

Inner chapel. Burning candles. Inner warmth. Smooth stone.

Leaf canopy. High windows. Sheltered balcony. Tended grave. Miniature tree. Wilting rose. Light drizzle. White flats. Pink anemone. Swaying poplar. Singing birds. Rumbling train.

Behind the clamour of the Wall Memorial, the calm of the Sophien cemetery.

Secluded spot. Old bench. Loving care. Empty flower pot.

Irrational wall. Arbitrary wall. Straight wall. Divisive wall. Everyday wall. Frustrating wall. Banal wall. Indifferent wall. Menacing wall. Annoying wall. Defaced wall. In place wall.

At places where bus routes were brought to an abrupt halt by the wall, there were large tarmaced circles so the buses could turn round. In Kleinmachnow, it is said, an irate driver once yanked his wheel so hard that it got stuck, and the bus travelled round in a circle for three days.

Irrational wall. Tortuous wall. Circular wall. Tall wall.

Orange coat. Blue folder. Black dog. Pink jacket. Blue jeans. Blonde hair. Stretched arms. Straight line. Smooth wall. Raised hands. Sincere gestures. Young learners.

Children are questioned about this ugly grey wall. When was it built? Who built it? Why was it built?

Simple questions. Raised hands. Young learners. Difficult answers.

WATERLOG

Vulgar errors
Pink bangles
Brampton urns
Brantano footwear
Marble brain
Alice bands
Urn burials
Biffa bin
Vulgar bangles
Plastercast skull
Yellow marigolds
Itinerant skull

Watching the
Thomas
Browne
memorial –
outsized
marble
eye

Illuminated interior
Plastic bangles
Hidden secrets
Vulgar bandanas

Extraordinary event
Unshapely hand
Significant date
Dead man's eyes
Thorough knowledge
Exposed tendons
Large canvas
Half-open mouth
Schematic plan
Deliberate intent
Amateur anatomist
Offending hand

Their gaze
is directed
just past it
to focus on
the open
anatomical
atlas

Archaic ritual
Punitive dimension
Reprobate body
Unshapely hand

Irreplaceable carpets
Embarrassed guide
Gilded mirrors
Dutch nef
Infinite view
Ornate ceiling
Clipped yew
Wrong turning
Soundproof toilet
Coronation chair
Old jelly beans
Squandered inheritance

Look at
this!
Look at
the view
up here!
How tall
are we?

Ancient maze
Incongruous portrait
Stuffed bear
Squandered inheritance

Old diesel
Threadbare seats
Gentle decline
Belching smokestack
Solitary cottage
Rippling reeds
Ruined buildings
Black smoke
Deserted platform
Social position
Whalebone corsets
Indestructible tweeds

So silent
that not
a word
might have
passed their lips
in the whole
of their lives

Ferny grotto
Silken tapestries
Golden pheasants
Belching smoke

Muddy track
Private estate
White petals
Withered ferns
Yellow digger
Feeding swans
Rising track
Fallen catkins
Glistening water
Fallen trunk
Rising wind
Distant laughter

Sunlight
through
the trees
Is that
water
or the
breeze?

Fallen trunk
Rushing water
Subsiding track
Kissing gate

Lost years
Wasted apprenticeship
Morning raids
Mind's eye
Enigmatic squadrons
German targets
Strange letters
Unfamiliar names
Key cities
Symbolic pictures
Tiny images
Romantic castles

The Eighth
Airfleet
alone
dropped seven hundred
and thirty-two
thousand tons
of bombs

Enigmatic land
Wasted land
Symbolic stamps
Lost years

Windy station
Deserted street
Empty hearse
Closed line
Icy drizzle
Rusting barge
Burning rubber
Torn flag
Deserted tennis courts
Lone surfer
Empty beach
Remaindered books

Even
Pound
World
here
has
shut
down

Empty hearse
Rusted exhaust
Deserted pier
Running dog

Superior description
Empty lobby
Echoing rooms
Startled woman
Narrow desk
Huge key
Wooden pear
Startled eye
Fixed gaze
Sole guest
Huge dining room
Gaudy wallpaper

A fish
that had
doubtless
lain entombed
in the
deep-freeze
for years

Thickening shadows
Scarlet blotches
Bay windows
White waves

Restless wind
Overgrown track
Yellow kayak
Crumbling cliff
Wet sand
Red pebble
Strong wind
Hovering gull
Red pebble
Empty beach
Brown pebble
Black dog

Streaming
clouds
at shoe
level –
wind
whipped
sand

Soaring oystercatcher
Thundering waves
Glistening pebbles
Yellow dog

Grassy dunes
Low cliffs
Tent-like shelters
Pebble beach
Regular intervals
Faraway lands
Taut lines
Immediate neighbourhood
Unfathomable feelings
Transistor radios
Thermos flasks
Abandoned boats

The last
stragglers
of some
nomadic people
at the
outermost limit
of the earth

High seas
Abandoned radios
Heavy skies
Salt air

Bare chest
White boat
Silver lamp-post
Children's cries
Deserted pavilion
Extinguished beacon
Circling gulls
Sheltering doves
Tall ferns
White feather
White pebble
Sea spray

In the middle
of nowhere
an abandoned
rucksack –
swimmers
in the
sea

Rusted winches
Circling gulls
Upturned tree-trunks
Dangerous cliffs

Angry sea
Becalmed waters
Coastal waters
Lightless depths
Vast shoals
Dependable sign
Large eye
Black pupil
Peculiar physiology
Flickering film
Black void
Women's hands

An idiosyncrasy
peculiar to
the herring
is that
when dead
it begins
to glow

White underbellies
Dependable sign
Flickering film
Powerful tail

Alphabetical flags
Numerical rags
Geometric flags
Coded flags
Medical assistance
Difficult manoeuvre
Urgent message
Serious fire
Yellow circle
Blue stripe
White strip
Yellow lozenge

You
should
stop
I have
something
important
to communicate

Extinguished lights
Starboard course
Stationary vessel
Serious fire

Heavy clouds
Dark cabin
Luminous rays
Tranquil sea
Western horizon
Dutch fleet
Drifting mists
First cannonades
Human figures
Smoking barrels
Tarred hulls
Acrid smoke

They would
have watched
the ships
moving hither
and thither
apparently
at random

Rare spectacle
Burning masts
Overcrowded decks
Drifting mists

Iron bridge
Narrow bridge
Sailing boat
Rotting barges
Grey water
Narrow-gauge railway
Local historians
Imperial train
Heraldic dragon
Black paintwork
Complete taxonomy
Subterranean treasures

According to
local historians
the train
had originally
been built
for the
Emperor of China

Oriental dragons
Blazing eyes
Seaside holidaymakers
Forbidden city

Missing bridge
Lost locomotive
Decisive moment
Opaque photograph
Initial puzzlement
Strange account
Known facts
Etymological proximity
Used post-cards
Lost nail-scissors
Imperial train
Tall tale

There
is no
train
and
there
never
was

Missing locomotive
Imperial post-cards
Lost bridge
Opaque holidaymakers

Forgotten footwear
Green bin
Mobile homes
Red boat
Shingle shore
Raised track
Lone jogger
Disused shed
Eroded soil
Worn track
Disused windmill
Wheeling gull

Silhouetted
on the
edge
of the
horizon
the dome of
Sizewell B

Twisting track
Waterlogged field
Silent marsh
Dangerous cliff

Profane power
Fibre-glass boat
Rotting barges
Purple-coloured walls
Lucrative ventures
Summer residences
Uncertain sources
Celestial capital
Starving peasants
Opium wars
Mass suicide
Last legs

His bloated
body
held together
only by
the silken
robes
of
imperial yellow

Immutable hierarchy
Free trade
Civilized progress
Moribund realm

Sunbathing seals
Revenant bittern
Silent swans
Gorse tunnel
Hovering sparrrowhawk
Curious fox
Sea lavender
Rising tide
Elevated hide
Empty canopy
Innumerable bulrushes
Nonchalant rabbits

Next
to
the
power
station –
abundance of
nature

Innumerable egrets
Nonchalant rabbits
Deserted beach
Incoming tide

Gentle breeze
Unfamiliar language
English tutors
Worldwide acclaim
Mohammedan uprising
Kaffir unrest
Indian troops
Largo Bay
Scottish emigrants
Motley assortment
Fair sex
Open fire

Her dress
onto which
she had
accidentally
spilt paraffin
caught
fire

Worldwide language
Unfamiliar breeze
Brass band
Open fire

Busy car park
Lost glove
Crumbling cliff
Sea swell
Friary ruin
Clipped hedge
Towering gorse
Open heath
Coiled hose
Frosty ground
Moss spore
Bird twitter

Listen
carefully
during the storm –
church bells
ringing
under
the sea

Smooth pole
Twisted trunk
Red heather
Black soil

Forlorn heath
Stunted pines
Melancholy region
Advancing destruction
Dense forests
Light soil
Strange luminescence
Still smoke
Great conflagration
Dry vegetation
Steep slopes
Agitated men

A little way off
from this scene
of devastation
a solitary man
with wild hair
was kneeling beside
his dead daughter

Pallid waters
Silting sands
Transparent ice
Swirling heath

Overgrown track
Curious neighbour
Small nettles
Diverted river
Mating dragonflies
Difficult track
Blue nettles
Lurking pike
Slow current
White butterfly
Giant nettles
Turning swan

Watching
the ground
at each
and every
step
to avoid
the nettles

Cool breeze
Bright clouds
Yellow lilies
Concealed nettles

Few memories
Dover customs
New identities
Berlin childhood
Dark corner
Mysterious sounds
Motor horns
Prussian nannies
Nauseating smell
Malt coffee
Cod liver oil
Silver bonbonniere

Were these not
all merely
phantasms
delusions
that had
dissolved
into thin air?

Leather seats
Baltic coast
Mysterious dunes
Pure sand

Peeling paint
Echoing voice
Warm glow
Open door
Bottle green
Black shadow
Green apple
Black file
Red apple
Opaque pane
Cluttered desk
Maritime sketch

The hand
rests on
the page
The eye
scans
the
line

Wooden ball
Empty box
Multi file
Illegible spine

Peaceful garden
Grey leaves
Mature willows
Deserted field
Soundless mouth
Flourishing bindweed
Yellow roots
Brown rot
Mental constructs
Old coat
Mental journeys
Dark grotto

A pot of tea
from which
there came
the occasional
puff of steam
as from
a toy engine

Old houses
Strange feeling
High ceiling
Soundless journeys

Silver birch
Embedded tyre
Scots pine
Concealed sign
Flat field
Distant shots
Hovering helicopter
Spent cartridge
Solemn memorial
Waterlogged meadow
Intermittent gunfire
Distant spire

The White House –
not destroyed
by a
doodlebug
just plain
old dry
rot

Hidden landrover
Loaded shotgun
High walls
Motionless pheasant

Vast properties
Huge plantations
Economic reasons
Lasting grievance
Two nations
Close connections
Ostentatious display
Accumulated wealth
Slave economy
Major auctions
Relentless escalation
Vast canvas

The curiously
close relationship
that existed
between the
history of sugar
and the
history of art

Secret methods
Arable land
Great oaks
Vast canvas

Martello tower
Shingle track
International school
Hidden park
Flat stone
Decaying groynes
Wave swell
Fallen pine
Overgrown paths
Inaccessible grottoes
Falling rocks
Exposed roots

Natural rock
formations
cast in
concrete
fissure and
fall away
revealing brick

Inaccessible grottoes
Crashing waves
Turreted roof
Desolate strand

Architectural marvel
Prominent site
Broad river
Imperial palace
Spectacular success
Entrepreneurial spirit
Convalescent holiday
Imperial majesties
Convalescence home
Barren land
Abandoned facilities
Abandoned spot

A demonstration
quite as unyielding
as the choice
of his heraldic motto
plutôt mourir que changer
which refuted
all compromise

Colossal manifestations
Convalescence home
Phosphorescent corpses
Special esteem

Long shadow
Carved tree
Glistening flint
White feather
Clear sky
Screeching tyre
Orange cartridge
Swaying pine
Distant shot
Grassy track
Deer print
Broken ice

Startled pheasants
burst into
the air
with an
explosion
of wings
and feathers

Glistening flint
Sandy track
Yellow cartridge
Distant cyclist

Long summer
Favourable conditions
Great wealth
Free enterprise
Legitimate position
Country mansion
Big business
Invited guests
Rural population
Secret colony
Breeding colony
Pheasant craze

They abandoned
the utilitarian principles
they had
always upheld
in favour
of hunting
and shooting

Staggering scores
Industrial scale
Big business
Symbolic bird

Stacked sand bags
Moving sail
Crunching gravel
Closed track
Fragile roof
Bearded reedling
Ballistic tables
Guided missiles
Otter prints
Camera obscura
Rare anemone
Collapsed building

Micro-organisms
carried by
the incoming
tide
into the heart
of the official
secrets act

Unexploded ordnance
Metamorphic pebbles
Ringed plover
Rusted wire

Secret research
Tarmac track
Quaking grass
Undiscovered country
Rough track
Paralysed state
Broad dyke
Gentle slopes
Dead arm
Meagre trickle
Concrete shells
Military installations

My sense
of being
on ground
intended for
purposes
transcending
the profane

Mysterious isle
Future catastrophe
Defunct machinery
Evening sun

Yellow primrose
Discreet bin
Black cap
Barking dog
Dry ditch
Electric fence
Still stream
Solitary bluebell
Broken stile
Enclosed field
Curious cows
Rapid retreat

Attracted by
the red
notebook
thirty-two
brown cows
stampede across
the field

Unforeseen detour
Sharp stone
Dangerous road
Abandoned spade

Roman road
Heavy sky
Dark islands
Harvested corn
Roman road
Billowing clouds
Red buses
Unending straight
Roman road
Sun's rays
Religious pictures
Brass knocker

I knew then
as little as
I know now
whether walking
in this solitary way
was more of a
pleasure or a pain

Roman road
Heavy sky
Dark islands
Harvested corn

Green overalls
Watchmaker's glasses
Arable fields
Temple precincts
Hard-gained insights
Squabbling scholars
Accurate replica
Evangelical sects
Archaeological experts
Television companies
Sacrificial altars
Covered walkways

We exchanged
a few words
of no consequence
as we walked to
the barn in
which the temple
was nearing completion

Accurate replica
Moonlit nights
Unheated barn
Divine revelation

Eccentric enquiry
Tall story
Ignored emails
Gravel drive
Unexpected enquiry
Tall hedge
Decorative logs
Pristine exterior
Deluded enquiry
Suspicious visitor
Drawn curtains
Unanswered phonecalls

There is
no moat
anywhere
to be seen
there is
no barn
no temple

Suspicious enquiry
Religious fanatic
Deluded fantasies
Closed gate

Still water
Steep bank
Flashing light
Melting ice
Grey sky
White line
Blue tractor
Blighted crops
Sunlit meadows
Worked-out soil
Frustrated farmers
White feathers

Through the
chink
in the
wooden
gates
what can
you see?

Stagnant water
Old tyres
Black pheasants
Round tower

Featureless plain
Remote livings
Mathematical theories
Immense forests
Growing fascination
Moral palor
Inner agitation
Untenable situation
Interminable play
Momentous upheavals
Fiery trajectories
Impossible theories

The chronicler
inscribes his
experiences
in an act of
self-mutilation
onto his
own body

Indelible ink
Surrounding heath
Solitary candle
Flickering fire

Piped music
Waterlogged field
Clipped conversation
Withered seed pod
Red wheelbarrow
Sculpted bark
Folded map
Concealed rod
Snapped pine
Steep climb
Wild garlic
Isolated lodge

Daffodils
in the
graveyard
compact
discs
in the
trees

Nervous pheasants
Clipped conversation
First primroses
Painted ceiling

Woeful events
Rapid decline
Heavy losses
Common species
Rapid summers
Marvellous light
Root systems
Green foliage
Entire avenues
Unbelievable speed
Tightened capillaries
Solitary trees

Within the space
of just two
or three summers
there were
no elms
left
alive

Infallible accuracy
Airborne beetles
Perfect trees
Immense space

Natural enemies
Ætherial salts
Brilliant night
Bononian stone
Sparkling constellations
Hebrew epistles
Equinoctial gales
Meticulous description
Empty horizon
Condensed air
Umbris Idæarum
Living truncation

A display
so resplendent
as I had
seen only
over the Alps
when I
was a child

Brilliant night
Empty horizon
Sparkling salt
Ætherial truncation

Invisible roads
Imagined destinations
Endless displacements
Futile quests
Invisible cul-de-sacs
Impenetrable signs
Inexhaustible tarmac
Vanishing pasts
Forgotten roads
Imaginary hopes
Lost traces
Closed doors

The
ultimate futility
of imagining
that treading in the steps
of an author
can illuminate
anything at all

Inexhaustible traces
Gathering dusk
Invisible pasts
Imaginary connections

AUTHOR'S NOTE

The poetic form used in these pages is one invented by Raymond Queneau in his 1975 book *Morale élémentaire*; it has come to be called the 'elementary morality' after this volume, or, after its inventor, the 'quennet', as it has one more line than a sonnet. David Bellos summarises the poem's structure in the following way:

> Three two-line stanzas, line 1 of each consisting of three phrases and line 2 of one phrase, each phrase formed by a noun-adjective pair
> *followed by*
> Seven lines of at least two and not more than seven syllables
> *followed by*
> One two-line stanza conforming to the same constraint as at the start.
>
> Rhymes, assonances, and repetitions between phrases and the 'middle lines' (what Queneau called the 'refrain') are not regulated but positively encouraged.

'Elementary Estuaries', a sequence based around estuary walks in Essex carried out between January 2006 and January 2007, at the rate of approximately one per week, uses Queneau's form relatively unchanged: the poem's appearance on the page, suggestive of receding flatnesses, seems perfectly adapted to the depiction of estuarine landscapes. The first set of two-line stanzas suggests the distant horizon, the refrain the watery middle-ground, the final two-line stanza the flat, and often muddy, foreground. Modelled, in part, on Georges Perec's *Les Lieux* project, for which he planned to visit twelve places in Paris twelve times each, ten estuaries, from the Stour to the Thames, were visited on five occasions each, giving a total of fifty poems – but the place of composition, for all these pieces were completed in the field, has not been attached to individual poems. Each piece, rather, remains untitled, detached from place, enabling the abstraction that Queneau's form can create to come into play. Poetry, since romanticism, has tended to privilege mountainous terrain, with the result that we have come to undervalue the stark beauties of fenland and marsh. In Essex, the result of this devaluation of the landscape has been particularly damaging, effectively offering developers and their bulldozers a *carte blanche.* The poems in 'Elementary Estuaries' try to let us see these flat yet rich landscapes afresh, defamiliarising them by use of periphrasis, close-up, recontextualisation, juxtaposition, and the quennet's typical recombination of the noun-adjective pairs in the final two-line stanzas. In this, the poems pay homage to a long tradition of nature writing, stretching from Thompson's *The Seasons* and Wordsworth and Coleridge's *Lyrical Ballads* to the work of poets like Peter Riley, Frances Presley and Tim Atkins in the present.

The second sequence of quennets is based on walks carried out between July 2007 and July 2009 round the 160-kilometre Berlin Wall Trail, or Mauerweg, and in the tradition of W. G. Sebald and Iain Sinclair it attempts to explore the psychogeography of the city. The Mauerweg is one of the achievements of Berlin's Social Democratic/ Green coalition of 2001–2. The original aim, which included putting all remaining traces of the wall under historic preservation orders, was to make the entire perimeter accessible to walkers and cyclists, an aim which was briefly achieved in 2005, though already, especially in the wealthier suburbs of the city, parts of the trail have been blocked and sectioned off, to be reincorporated into private parks and gardens, or earmarked for development. Originally, these poems were begun using the same form as 'Elementary Estuaries', but I quickly realised this wasn't working – Queneau's original form is too open, too playful even, for what were essentially poems about a political boundary and Cold War enclosure. Consequently, the form was adapted into a wall-like block of prose, but a block of prose that was nevertheless fractured by the refrain, suggesting the collapse of the wall in 1989 and the new vistas opened up by this momentous event.

The final sequence of poems, 'Waterlog', which retraces the steps of W. G. Sebald through Suffolk, as recorded in *The Rings of Saturn,* demanded yet another adaptation of Queneau's form. Here, influenced by the walk poems of Richard Long, the quennet is stretched out to give a long, thin poem. The wide, unjustified right-hand margin deliberately mirrors the eroding effects of the sea on the Suffolk coastline near towns like Dunwich, now partly submerged beneath the waves, the words clinging to the edge of the page like houses to a threatened cliff top, while the text here is itself partly made up of fragments of Sebald's writing, as if his work had also been subject to erosion. This potential for the quennet to reconfigure text borrowed from literary source material was seen early on by the Oulipo, who have published quennets collaging text derived from such sources, including Queneau's novels, in the *Bibliothèque Oulipienne*. At the same time, the straightness of the poem mirrors the often linear nature of Sebald's perigrinations, though at times, it must be said, the paths Sebald follows are far from straight, and often discontinuous, just as the stories he recounts, while sometimes straight, are just as often tangential, barbed and unreliable, at times branching into pure fiction. While Sebald asserts that the White House at Bredfield in Suffolk where the writer Edward Fitzgerald was born on 31 March 1809 was 'levelled to the ground in May 1944 when one of the German V-bombs, which the English nicknamed 'doodlebugs', suddenly deviated from its course', the local postmaster confidently assured me that the real cause of damage was dry-rot. Similarly, when Sebald asserts that the train which ran from Halesworth to Southwold 'had originally been built for the Emperor of China', a connection which facilitates a long digression on the last days of imperial China, there is no factual basis for his claims. Such findings, and many others, work their way into the poems, which at once retrace and interrogate Sebald's steps.

Philip Terry, May 2016

ACKNOWLEDGEMENTS

The confluence of ideas and approaches which made this book possible – ideas from Oulipo, from land art, from psychogeography, from nature writing, and from experimental poetry – were a direct result of the work I was engaged in with colleagues at the University of Essex at the time of writing, in particular the Memory Maps project, convened by Marina Warner. I would like to thank all my friends and colleagues from the University of Essex, in particular Marina Warner, Adrian May and James Canton, as well as the many inspirational guests we invited to our yearly colloquia, Ken Worpole, Rachel Lichtenstein, Mark Cocker, Helen Macdonald, and Iain Sinclair, amongst others, without whose example and guidance these poems would not have been written. The V&A, who generously hosted the Memory Maps website, and where I was able to experiment with some early drafts of these quennets, also deserves my special thanks.